YOUR KNOWLEDGE HAS

Bibliographic information published by the German National Library:

The German National Library lists this publication in the National Bibliography; detailed bibliographic data are available on the Internet at http://dnb.dnb.de .

Imprint:

Copyright © 2013 GRIN Verlag, Open Publishing GmbH
Print and binding: Books on Demand GmbH, Norderstedt Germany
ISBN: 9783656411871

This book at GRIN:

http://www.grin.com/en/e-book/212932/comparative-analysis-between-grid-and-cloud-computing

Bijoy Boban

Comparative analysis between Grid and Cloud computing

GRIN Publishing

GRIN - Your knowledge has value

Since its foundation in 1998, GRIN has specialized in publishing academic texts by students, college teachers and other academics as e-book and printed book. The website www.grin.com is an ideal platform for presenting term papers, final papers, scientific essays, dissertations and specialist books.

Visit us on the internet:

http://www.grin.com/

http://www.facebook.com/grincom

http://www.twitter.com/grin_com

A COMPARATIVE ANALYSIS BETWEEN

CLOUD COMPUTING AND GRID COMPUTING.

Er. Bijoy Boban (Reg No: 11200402, Roll No: A09)
Lovely Institute of Technology and Sciences (School: K2, Session: 209)
Lovely Professional University
Phagwara, India-144411
April 2013

Abstract -Cloud computing is the current most trendy and social technology that has been launched on the network world which can also be called as a reincarnation or evolution of Grid computing, so the Clouds are considered as a new generation of Grid computing. These Clouds consist of data centres which are owned by individual institute, organisations or companies. The homogeneity within each data centre in the infrastructure is the main feature for the cloud computing compared to grid computing. Cloud Computing has become another most used word on internet after Web 2.0. There are many definitions for Cloud computing and there seems to be no consensus on what a Cloud is. Cloud Computing is not a completely new concept, it has intricate connection to the relatively new but thirteen year established Grid Computing paradigm and other relevant technologies such as utility computing, cluster computing, and distributed systems when we go through the structure and working of a Cloud.

Keywords- Cloud computing, Grid computing, SAAS (Software As A Service), IAAS (Infrastructure As A Service), PAAS (Platform As A Service).

I. INTRODUCTION

In this paper we give a comparative analysis between the latest in market Cloud computing and the famous through Google architecture, the back born of Google networks, the Grid computing. Cloud computing emerged as one of the trend setting and speed oriented technology in networks. Cloud computing is made with the logical and physical combination of many other sectors of computing technology such as HPC, virtualization, utility computing and grid computing, so as we said in the abstract cloud was an evolution from grid computing. In order to make clear the importance of cloud computing, we are giving a detailed description of the characteristics of this area which make cloud computing being cloud computing and distinguish it from other research areas like grid computing. The main characteristics of cloud computing that make it distinct from others are service oriented, loose coupling, strong fault

tolerant, business model and easily usable by any internet user. Now let us consider grid computing at the other end, Grid computing in the simplest case refers to cooperation of multiple processors on multiple machines and its objective is to boost the computational power in the fields which require high capacity of the CPU [3]. In grid computing multiple servers which use common operating systems and software have interactions with each other. Grid computing is hardware and software infrastructure which offer a cheap, distributable, coordinated and reliable access to powerful computational capabilities, i.e. why grid computing stayed in the market for over 14 years and still under use.

From the overview on the above explanations we can say that Cloud Computing represents a novel and promising approach for implementing scalable ICT systems for individuals, communities and business use, relying on the latest achievements of diverse research areas such as Grid computing, Service oriented computing, business processes and virtualization. From the technological point of view Grid computing is considered as the most related predecessor technology of Cloud computing. Although Cloud and Grid computing differ in many aspects, as for example in the general idea of the provision of computational resource which is in Clouds commercial based and in Grids community based there are many similarities. In this term paper we investigate the similarities and differences between Clouds and Grids by evaluating two successful projects and also evaluating various features, fault tolerance, security, service and other aspects.

II. CLOUD, GRID AND DISTRIBUTED SYSTEM

You might have immediately notice that our definition of Cloud Computing overlaps with many existing technologies such as Grid Computing, Utility Computing, Services

Computing, and distributed computing in general. We argue that Cloud Computing not only overlaps with Grid Computing, it is indeed evolved out of Grid Computing and relies on Grid Computing as its backbone and infrastructure support. The evolution has been a result of a shift in focus from an infrastructure that delivers storage and compute resources (such is the case in Grids) to one that is economy based aiming to deliver more abstract resources and services (such is the case in Clouds). As for Utility Computing, it is not a new paradigm of computing infrastructure; rather, it is a business model in which computing resources, such as computation and storage, are packaged as metered services similar to a physical public utility, such as electricity and public switched telephone network. Utility computing is typically implemented using other computing infrastructure (e.g. Grids) with additional accounting and monitoring services. A Cloud infrastructure can be utilized internally by a company or exposed to the public as utility computing. See Figure 1 for an overview of the relationship between Clouds and other domains that it overlaps with. Web 2.0 covers almost the whole spectrum of service-oriented applications, where Cloud Computing lies at the large-scale side. Supercomputing and Cluster Computing have been more focused on traditional non-service applications. Grid Computing overlaps with all these fields where it is generally considered of lesser scale than supercomputers and Clouds [2].

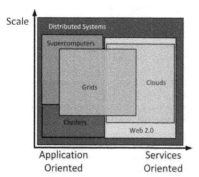

Figure 1: Grids and Clouds Overview [2]

Grid Computing aims to enable resource sharing and coordinated problem solving in dynamic, multi-institutional virtual organizations [12][13]. There are also a few key features to this definition: First of all, Grids provide a distributed computing

paradigm or infrastructure that spans across multiple virtual organizations (VO) where each VO can consist of either physically distributed institutions or logically related projects/groups. The goal of such a paradigm is to enable federated resource sharing in dynamic, distributed environments. The approach taken by the *de facto* standard implementation – The Globus Toolkit [14][15], is to build a uniform computing environment from diverse resources by defining standard network protocols and providing middleware to mediate access to a wide range of heterogeneous resources. Globus addresses various issues such as security, resource discovery, resource provisioning and management, job scheduling, monitoring, and data management. Half a decade ago, Ian Foster gave a three point checklist [16] to help define what is, and what not a Grid is:

❖ Coordinates resources that are not subject to centralized control,
❖ Uses standard, open, general-purpose protocols and interfaces.
❖ Delivers non-trivial qualities of service. Although point 3 holds true for Cloud Computing, neither point 1 nor point 2 is clear that it is the case for today's Clouds.

The vision for Clouds and Grids are similar, details and technologies used may differ, but the two communities are struggling with many of the same issues. This paper strives to compare and contrast Cloud Computing with Grid Computing from various angles and give insights into the essential characteristics of both, with the hope to paint a less cloudy picture of what Clouds are, what kind of applications can Clouds expect to support, and what challenges Clouds are likely to face in the coming years as they gain momentum and adoption. We hope this will help both communities gain deeper understanding of the goals, assumptions, status, and directions, and provide a more detailed view of both technologies to the general audience.

III. CLOUD DEFINITION

As Cloud is new and as Cloud is not under any proprietary ownership or organisation, people who devote or contribute to the development of cloud gives their own definition based up on service at various levels or according to architectural basis they have developed. So there is no standard or agreed definition for Cloud. According to Gartner [5], Cloud computing is a style of computing where massively scalable IT related capabilities are provided as a service across the cyber infrastructure to external users. It has been claimed for some aspects that cloud systems are narrow Grids, in the sense of exposing reduced interfaces.

Table 1: reference as extracted from [6].

Author/Reference	Year	Definition/Excerpt
M. Klems	2008	you can scale your infrastructure on demand within minutes or even seconds, instead of days or weeks, thereby avoiding under-utilization (idle servers) and over-utilization (blue screen) of in-house resources...
P. Gaw	2008	using the internet to allow people to access technology-enabled services. Those services must be 'massively scalable...
R. Buyya	2008	A Cloud is a type of parallel and distributed system consisting of a collection of interconnected and virtualized computers that are dynamically provisioned and presented as one or more unified computing resources based on service-level agreements established through negotiation between the service provider and consumers
R. Cohen	2008	Cloud computing is one of those catch all buzz words that tries to encompass a variety of aspects ranging from deployment, load balancing, provisioning, business model and architecture (like Web2.0). It's the next logical step in software (software 10.0). For me the simplest explanation for Cloud Computing is describing it as, "internet centric software...
J. Kaplan	2008	a broad array of web-based services aimed at allowing users to obtain a wide range of functional capabilities on a 'pay-as-you-go' basis that previously required tremendous hardware/ software investments and professional skills to acquire. Cloud computing is the realization of the earlier ideals of utility computing without the technical complexities or complicated deployment worries...
D. Edwards	2008	...what is possible when you leverage web-scale infrastructure (application and physical) in an on-demand way...
K. Sheynkman	2008	Clouds focused on making the hardware layer consumable as ondemand compute and storage capacity. This is an important first step, but for companies to harness the power of the Cloud, complete application infrastructure needs to be easily configured, deployed, dynamically-scaled and managed in these virtualized hardware environments

IV. CLOUD COMPUTING MODEL

IV.1 DEPLOYMENT MODEL

This is a new model concept that can be divided into the following four famous models (but there might be other models that can be drawn from them) [10]:

- ❖ Public: Services and resources are reachable to the public by using the internet. This environment emphasises the advantages of rationalization (as a user has the ability to utilize only the needed services and pay only for their use), operational simplicity (as the system is organized and hosted by a third party) and scalability. The main concern in this type of cloud environment is the security; since this environment is accessible to the public and user data in one stage is hosted by a third party [1].

- ❖ Private: Services and resources are reachable within a private institute. This environment emphasises the advantages of integration, optimization of hardware deals and scalability. The main concern is the complexity, as this environment is organized and hosted by internal resources. Security is not a main issue compared to the public cloud as the services are reachable only through private and internal networks [2].

- ❖ Community: Services and resources of this type are shared by various institutes with a common aim. It may be organized by one of the institutes or a third party [7].

- ❖ Hybrid: This type combines the methods from the private and public clouds, where resources can be used either in a public or a private cloud environment [8]. The advantages and the concerns are a mixture of the earlier type. Another cloud technology which has become very popular recently is called Green Cloud Computing. Its aim is to reduce resource consumption and yet fulfil quality of service needed and hold the resources switched off as long as possible. "The advantages of such technology are lower heat production and power saving by employing server consolidation and virtualization technologies; since active resources (servers, network elements, and A/C units) that are idle lead to energy waste" [9].

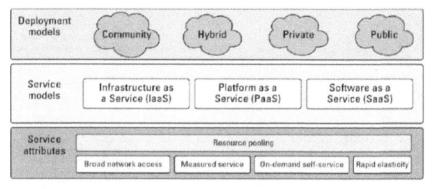

Figure 2: The NIST cloud computing definitions [3].

IV.2 SERVICE MODEL

Infrastructure-as-a-Service is the delivery of huge computing resources such as the capacity of processing, storage and network. Taking storage as an example, when a user use the storage service of cloud computing, he just pay the consuming part without buying any disks or even knowing nothing about the location of the data he deals with. Sometimes the IaaS is also called Hardware-as-a-Service (HaaS) [17] [18]. Platform-as-a-Service generally abstracts the infrastructures and supports a set of application program interface to cloud applications. It is the middle bridge between hardware and application. Because of the importance of platform, many big companies want to grasp the chance of pre-dominating the platform of cloud computing as Microsoft does in personal computer time. The well known examples are Google App Engine [19] and Microsoft's Azure Services Platform [20]. Software-as-a-Service aims at replacing the applications running on PC. There is no need to install and run the special software on your computer if you use the SaaS. Instead of buying the software at a relative higher price, you just follow the pay-per-use pattern which can reduce you total cost. The concept of SaaS is attractive and some software runs well as cloud computing, but the delay of network is fatal to real time or half real time applications such as 3D online game.

V. CLOUD ARCHITECTURE

Clouds computing could be comprised of several heterogeneous components/systems such as grids computing, cluster, super computers etc. (Figure 3). This aggregation is used by millions of users. Consider, for example the case of Microsoft's Live, where the system has around 300 million users. Added to this, there are almost 330.000 application developers of Amazon EC2. Cloud Architecture consists of software

applications, which use Internet-accessible on-demand services. Therefore, these applications are considered as an essential computing infrastructure that is used when it is required (such as processing a user request) and to perform a specific job by giving up unwanted resources. Also drawing the needed resources on demand (like compute servers or storage).

There are some difficulties of large-scale data processing that are addressed by cloud architecture.

❖ First of all, it is difficult to increase the number of machines to reach an application requirement.
❖ It is not easy to achieve the machines when needed by any application.
❖ It is complex to distribute and organize a large-scale job on different machines for example running processes on them and provision another machine to recover if one of them stops working.
❖ It is hard to dispose of all those machines when the job is completed.
❖ It is difficult to auto scale up and down based on dynamic workloads. These problems have been solved by cloud architectures.

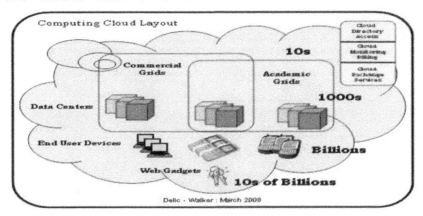

Figure 3. Computing Cloud, Source: [12]

Plenty of applications may be effective because they utilize the power of the cloud Architectures. Some of these applications are widely and frequently used, for instance Processing Pipelines (Video trans coding pipelines – trans code AVI to

MPEG movies), Batch Processing Systems (Log analysis – analyze and generate daily/weekly reports) and Websites (Seasonal Websites).

VI. GRID COMPUTING

While still there are several different conceptions upon the definition of the grids Ian Foster has indicate [21] a definition of the Grid as a system that coordinates resources which are not subject to centralized control, using standard, open, general-purpose protocols and interfaces to deliver nontrivial qualities of service. Nowadays, it can be clearly observed that Clouds are the latest paradigm to emerge that promises reliable services delivered through next-generation data centres which are built on virtualized compute and storage technologies [22]. The popularity of different paradigms varies with time. The web search popularity, as measured by the Google search trends during the last 12 months, for terms cluster computing, Grid computing, and Cloud computing is shown in Figure 4. From the Google trends, it can be observed that cluster computing was a popular term during 1990s, from early 2000 Grid computing become popular, and recently Cloud computing started gaining popularity [23].

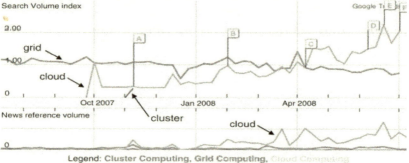

Figure 4: Google search trends for the last 12 months. Source [23]

The following points are adopted from [23]:

Spot points in this figure indicate the release of news related to Cloud computing as follows:

* IBM Introduces 'Blue Cloud' Computing, CIO Today - Nov 15 2007.
* IBM, EU Launch RESERVOIR Research Initiative for Cloud Computing, IT News Online Feb 7 2008.
* Google and Salesforce.com in Cloud computing deal, Siliconrepublic.com - Apr 14 2008.
* Demystifying Cloud Computing, Intelligent Enterprise - Jun 11 2008.
* Yahoo realigns to support Cloud computing, 'core strategies', San Antonio Business Journal Jun 27 2008.
* Merrill Lynch Estimates "Cloud Computing" To Be $100 Billion Market, SYS-CON Media Jul 8 2008.

VII GRID ARCHITECTURE

Amadeus. Figure 5 shows the architecture of the Amadeus environment used to manage execution of Grid workflows. Amadeus has been successfully utilized for the provision and management of HPC applications as for example maxillo facial surgery application used in medical practice for preparation of medical treatments [25]. The main components include

* A Visualization and Specification component.
* A Planning, Negotiation and Execution component called QoS-aware Grid Workflow Engine (QWE), and
* A set of Grid Resources.

The specification and visualization component comprises a tool for UML based Grid workflow modelling and visualization. A user may specify the workflow by composing predefined workflow elements. For each workflow element different properties (such as execution time, price and location affinity) may be specified that indicate the user's QoS requirements. After the validation of the specified workflow, a corresponding XML representation is generated following the syntax of QoWL [24]. The QWE engine interprets the QoWL workflow, applies the selected optimization strategy, negotiates with services, selects appropriate services and finally executes the workflow. The requested QoS and the negotiated QoS may be expressed using a language for the specification of electronic contracts, as for example Web Service Level Agreement (WSLA). For the activities annotated with QoS constraints, we use QoS aware services (i.e., Vienna Grid Environment (VGE) services), which are able to provide certain QoS guarantees. For other activities non-VGE services may be used.

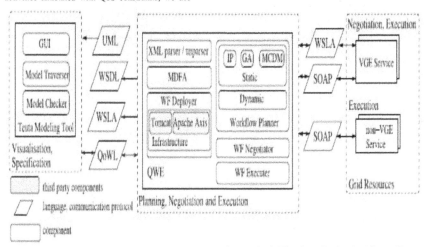

Figure 5: Amadeus architecture (grid) [5].

VIII. COMPARISON

Viewed in a broad sense, the concepts of grid and cloud computing seems to have similar features. This section puts light to differentiate in different perspectives and give an end-to-end comparison. It could be understood easily when represented in a tabular form as given in table 1 [3].

One indicator of the buzz or hype of a particular technology can be examined by the search volume of keywords in popular search engines. Google has just this type of tool with their Google Trends. With this tool, we can compare different search terms against each other and view how the search volume changes over time. The Google trends showed in Figure 4 bottom part. In red is Grid Computing and in blue is Cloud Computing. If we now compare Cloud Computing against Dedicated Server and Virtualization, figure 4 top part is the result. Here in blue is Cloud Computing, in red is Grid computing, in orange is Dedicated server, and in green is Virtualization[3]. The cloud is the same basic idea as the grid, but scaled down in some ways, scaled up in others, and thoroughly democratized. Like the grid, the cloud is a utility computing model that involves a dynamically growing and shrinking collection of heterogeneous, loosely coupled nodes, all of which are aggregated together and present themselves to a client as a single pool of compute and/or storage resources. But though the server side of the model may look similar, most the major differences between cloud and grid stem from the differences between their respective clients. Instead of a few clients running massive, multimode jobs, the cloud services thousands or millions of clients, typically serving multiple clients per node. These clients have small, fleeting tasks e.g., database queries or HTTP requests that are often computationally very lightweight but possibly storage or bandwidth intensive. (Figure 5). See Figure 5 for an overview of the relationship between Clouds and other domains that it overlaps with [3]. Web 2.0 covers almost the whole spectrum of service-oriented applications, where Cloud Computing lies at the large scale side. Grid computing overlaps with all these fields where it is generally considered of lesser scale than supercomputers and Clouds. Some of the applications and tools in grid computing and cloud computing are briefed here (see table 2 and 3) [3].

Table 1: *GC Vs. CC*

Parameter	Grid computing	Cloud computing
Goal	Collaborative sharing of resources	Use of service (eliminates the detail)
Computational focuses	Computationally intensive operations	Standard and high-level instances
Workflow management	In one physical node	In EC2 instance (Amazon EC2+S3)
Level of abstraction	Low (more details)	High (eliminate details)
Degree of scalability	Normal	High
Multitask	Yes	Yes
Transparency	Low	High
Time to run	Not real-time	Real-time services
Requests type	Few but large allocation	Lots of small allocation
Allocation unit	Job or task (small)	All shapes and sizes (wide & narrow)
Virtualization	Not a commodity	Vital
Portal accessible	Via a DNS system	Only using IP (no DNS registered)
Transmission	Suffered from internet delays	Was significantly fast
Security	Low (grid certificate service)	High (Virtualization)
Infrastructure	Low level command	High level services (SaaS)
Operating System	Any standard OS	A hypervisor (VM) on which multiple OSs run
Ownership	Multiple	Single
Interconnection network	Mostly internet with latency and low bandwidth	Dedicated, high-end with low latency and high bandwidth
Discovery	Centralized indexing and decentralized info services	Membership services
Service negotiation	SLA based	SLA based
User management	Decentralized and also Virtual Organization (VO)-based	Centralized or can be delegated to third party
Resource management	Distributed	Centralized/Distributed
Allocation/Scheduling	Decentralized	Both centralized/decentralized
Interoperability	Open grid forum standards	Web Services (SOAP and REST)
Failure management	Limited (often failed tasks/applications are restarted)	Strong (VMs can be easily migrated from one node to other)

Pricing of services	Dominated by public good or privately assigned	Utility pricing, discounted for larger customers
User friendly	Low	High
Type of service	CPU, network, memory, bandwidth, device, storage,...	IaaS, PaaS, SaaS, Everything as a service
Data intensive storage	Suited for that	Not suited for that
Example of real world	SETI, BOINC, Folding@home, GIMPS	Amazon Web Service (AWS), Google apps
Response Time	Can't be serviced at a time and need to be scheduled	Real-time
Critical object	Computer resource	Service
Number of users	Few	More
Resource	Limited (because hardware are limited)	Unlimited
Configuration	Difficult as users haven't administrator privilege	Very easy to configure
Future	Cloud computing	Next generation of internet

IX. MAJOR DIFFERENCES BETWEEN

GRID AND CLOUD

In the following we summarize the major differences between Grids and Clouds.

Business Models. While in Grid business models are usually based on bilateral agreements between academic institutions, provision of resource in Clouds requires more differentiated business models as discussed next. Currently, we observe several types of business models ranging from resource providers who only provide computing resources (e. g., Amazon, Tsunamic Technologies), over SaaS providers who sell their own resources together with their own software services (e. g., GoogleApps, Salesforce.com) to companies that attempt to run a mixed approach, i. e., they allow users to create their own services but at the same time offer their own services (Sun N1 Grid, Microsoft Azure).

Resource Management. Resource management represents another major difference between Grids and Clouds. While Grids rely on batch systems, utilization of virtualization technologies represents the resource management solution for the Clouds.

Resource Provision Models. As already discussed in previous sections Grid resource provisioning models are based on virtual organisations where the relationships are established offline. In Clouds usage of SLAs, compliance, and trust management is essential.

Resource Availability. In Grids resource sharing relies on the best effort manner, sometimes resources are not available and sometimes there are plenty of resources which are idle. Clouds rely on massive elasticity in Clouds. Challenging issues in Clouds are to find the balance between wasting resources due to the virtualization overhead and standby modes of devices on the one hand, and pooling of resources to facilitate efficient consumption of resources and reducing energy consumption on the other.

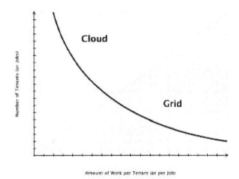

Figure 4: Scale comparison

Figure 6 [3]:

Table 2: Grid and Cloud applications

Technology	Application	Comment
Grid	DDGrid (Drug Discovery Grid)	This project aims to build a collaboration platform for drug discovery using the state-of-the-art P2P and grid computing technology [27].
	MammoGrid	It is a service-oriented architecture based medical grid application [26].
	Geodise	Geodise aims to provide a Grid-based generic integration framework for computation and data intensive multidisciplinary design optimization tasks.
Cloud	Cloudo	A free computer that lives on the Internet, right in the web browser.
	RoboEarth	Is a European project led by the Eindhoven University of Technology, Netherlands, to develop a WWW for robots, a giant database where robots can share information about objects [28].
	Panda Cloud antivirus	The first free antivirus from the cloud [29].

Table 3: Grid and Cloud tools

Technology	Tool	Comment
Grid	Nimrod-G	Uses the Globus middleware services for dynamic resource discovery and dispatching jobs over computational grids [30].
	Gridbus	(GRID computing and BUSiness) toolkit project is associated with the design and development of cluster and grid middleware technologies for service oriented computing [31].
	Legion	Is an object-based meta-system that supports transparent core scheduling, data management, fault tolerance, site autonomy, and a middleware with a wide range of security options [32].
Cloud	Cloudera	An open-source Hadoop software framework is increasingly used in cloud computing deployments due to its flexibility with cluster-based, data intensive queries and other tasks [33].
	CloudSim	Important for developers to evaluate the requirements of large-scale cloud applications.
	Zenoss	A single, integrated product that monitors the entire IT infrastructure, wherever it is deployed (physical, virtual, or in cloud).

X. CONCLUSION

In this paper, we have presented a detailed comparison on the two computing models, grid and cloud computing. We believe a close comparison such as this can help the two communities understand, share and evolve infrastructure and technology within and across, and accelerate Cloud Computing from early prototypes to production systems. When it comes to grid and cloud computing, the two are often seen as the same computing paradigm under different names. In this paper, we sought to separate grids from clouds and provide a side by side comparison in how they are assembled and what services are offered. In a word, the concept of cloud computing is becoming more and more popular. Now cloud computing is in the beginning stage. All kinds of companies are providing all kinds of cloud computing service, from software application to net storage and mail filter. We believe cloud computing will become main technology in our information life. Cloud has owned all the conditions. Now the dream of grid computing will be realized by cloud computing. It will be a great event in the IT history. Grid and cloud computing appears to be a promising model especially focusing on standardizing APIs, security, interoperability, new business models, and dynamic pricing systems for complex services. Hence there is a scope for further research in these areas.

REFERENCES

[1] COMPARISON BETWEEN CLOUD AND GRID COMPUTING: REVIEW PAPER Hosam AlHakami, Hamza Aldabbas, and Tariq Alwada'n Software Technology Research Laboratory (STRL), De Montfort University, Leicester, United Kingdom {hosam, hamza, tariq}@dmu.ac.uk

[2] Cloud Computing and Grid Computing 360-Degree Compared 1,2,3Ian Foster, 4Yong Zhao, 1Ioan Raicu, 5Shiyong Lu foster@mcs.anl.gov, yozha@microsoft.com, iraicu@cs.uchicago.edu, shiyong@wayne.edu 1. Department of Computer Science, University of Chicago, Chicago, IL, USA 2. Computation Institute, University of Chicago, Chicago, IL, USA 3.Math & Computer Science Division, Argonne National Laboratory, Argonne, IL, USA 4. Microsoft Corporation, Redmond, WA, USA 5. Department of Computer Science, Wayne State University, Detroit, MI, USA

[3] Cloud Computing Vs. Grid Computing 1Seyyed Mohsen Hashemi, 2Amid Khatibi Bardsiri 1. Dean of the Software Engineering and Artificial Intelligence Department , Science and Research Branch, Islamic Azad University, Tehran, IRAN 2. Computer Engineering Department, Bardsir Branch, Islamic Azad University, Kerman, IRAN

Email: {hashemi@isrup.com,
a.khatibi@srbiau.ac.ir}

[4] Grid vs Cloud – A Technology Comparison Grid vs Cloud – Ein Technologischer Vergleich Ivona Brandic, Schahram Dustdar, Vienna University of Technology.

[5] R. Desisto, D. Plummer, Smith(2007). "Tutorial for Understanding the Relationship Between Cloud Computing and SaaS". http://www.gartner.com/DisplayDocument?ref=g_s earch\&id=640707

[6] L. M. Vaquero, L. R. Merino , J. Caceres, M Lindner. (2009). "A Break in the Clouds: Towards a Cloud Definition". http://portal.acm.org/citation.cfm?id=1496091.149 6100

[7] Mell, P., Grance, T.: The nist definition of cloud computing (draft) recommendations of the national institute of standards and technology. Nist Special Publication 145(6), 7 (2011), http://csrc.nist.gov/publications/ drafts/800-145/Draft-SP-800-145_cloud-definition.pdf.

[8] Sotomayor, B., Montero, R.S., Llorente, I.M., Foster, I.: Virtual infrastructure management in private and hybrid clouds. IEEE Internet Computing 13, 14–22 (September 2009), http://dl.acm.org/citation.cfm?id= 1638588.1638692

[9] Werner, J., Geronimo, G., Westphall, C., Koch, F., Freitas, R.: Simulator improvements to validate the green cloud computing approach. In: Network Operations and Management Symposium (LANOMS), 2011 7th Latin American. pp. 1 –8 (oct 2011).

[10] De Chaves, S.A., Uriarte, R.B., Westphall, C.B.: Toward an architecture for monitoring private clouds. IEEE Communications Magazine 49(12), 130–137 (2011), http://dblp.unitrier. de/db/journals/cm/ cm49.html#ChavesUW11.

[11] K. A. Delic and M. A. Walker. (2008) ." Emergence of The Academic Computing Clouds".

http://www.acm.org/ubiquity/volume_9/v9i31_deli c.html

[12] I. Foster, C. Kesselman, S. Tuecke. The anatomy of the Grid: Enabling scalable virtual organization. The Intl. Jrnl. of High Performance Computing Applications, 15(3):200--222, 2001.

[13] I. Foster, C. Kesselman, J. Nick, S. Tuecke. The Physiology of the Grid: An Open Grid Services Architecture for Distributed Systems Integration. Globus Project, 2002.

[14] I. Foster, C. Kesselman. "Globus: A Metacomputing Infrastructure Toolkit", Intl J. Supercomputer Applications, 11(2):115-128, 1997.

[15] I. Foster. "Globus Toolkit Version 4: Software for Service- Oriented Systems." IFIP Int. Conf. on Network and Parallel Computing, Springer-Verlag LNCS 3779, pp 2-13, 2006.

[16] I. Foster. What is the Grid? A Three Point Checklist, July 2002.

[17] ."What is cloud computing?" http://searchcloudcomputing.techtarget.com/sDefin iti on/0sid201gci1287881,00.html.

[18] .L.M. Vaquero, L.R. Merino, J. Caceres, and M. Lindner, "A break in the clouds: towards a cloud definition," ACM SIGCOMM Computer Communication Review, Vol. 39, No. 1, 2009.

[19].Google, "Google app Engine," http://code.google.com/appengine/.

[20].Microsoft, "Windows Azure", http://www.microsoft.com/windows azure.

[21] I. Foster(2002). What is the Grid? A Three Point Checklist. Grid Today, vol. 1, no. 6, pp. 22 25.

[22] A. Weiss. (2007). Computing in the Clouds, netWorker 11 (4) 16_25

[23] R. Buyya, C. S. Yeoa, S. Venugopala, J. Broberg, I. Brandic. (2008). "Cloud computing and emerging IT platforms: Vision, hype, and reality for delivering computing as the 5th utility". Journal homepage: www.elsevier.com/locate/fgcs

[24] I. Brandic, S. Benkner, G. Engelbrecht, and R. Schmidt. QoS Support for Time-Critical Grid Workflow Applications. In: Proc. of the 1st IEEE Int'l Conf. on eScience and Grid Computing, Melbourne, Australia, Dec 2005.

[25] I. Brandic, S. Pllana, and S. Benkner.
Specification, Planning, and Execution of QoS-
aware Grid Workflows within the Amadeus
Environment. In: Concurrency and Computation:
Practice and Experience 20(4):331–345, Mar 2008.

YOUR KNOWLEDGE HAS VALUE

- We will publish your bachelor's and
  master's thesis, essays and papers

- Your own eBook and book -
  sold worldwide in all relevant shops

- Earn money with each sale

Upload your text at www.GRIN.com
and publish for free